THIS PLANNER BELONGS TO:

____

The Backyard Bird Planner

Amy Tan

Clarkson Potter/Publishers
New York

Every Day Is a Chance to Discover Something New

As a fiction writer, I typically spend hours in my imagination, where clocks don't exist, and real time passes from evening to morning as if only an hour has gone by. But at one time, I was a freelance business writer with twelve-hour days crammed into thirty-minute increments of billable time, client meetings, multiple deadlines, and squeezed-in appointments for dental cleaning, car repairs, or occasional dinner dates. I was productive and punctual. Meeting the priorities of others was my goal. One day, I finally picked up a novel again. It was like being reunited with an old friend. The more I read, the more inspired I was to write my own stories. I reflected on my past, what I believed and why, and that led to the deep and endless question: "What does it mean to be truly alive?" I set out to find the answers.

I've always wanted a planner that allows for more freedom and flexibility for organizing a fulfilling life. I finally created one that I think is especially useful for those who have creative aspirations. It can note each day's responsibilities, alongside reminders to wander and wonder. There is also a place on the page to articulate professional and personal goals, which can help you see the connections between how we spend our time and how we create our lives. I've even included a rest stop, where you can take time in your day to notice and reflect.

Being intentionally curious can lead you to discover something new every day. Discovery is what made childhood so exciting. And the best way to do that is to step outdoors, where you can immerse yourself in nature. There is real science behind the calming and restorative benefits of being in the wild for even five minutes. As you can guess, I've found birds are excellent guides to wonder, hope, and joy. Watch until you see what you've never noticed before. How birds hunt for food, or how they guard it or share it with fledglings or prospective mates. Listen to the differences in birdsongs and try to imitate them. Think about the life of a bird and yours, its emotions and yours, its will to survive and yours. Allow yourself the time to live deeply in nature.

To begin, take five minutes to reflect on life all around you, then grow from there with small discoveries. Start your day by noticing a bird and seeing if it notices you. Restore yourself with a forest bath during a windy lunch hour. Step away from the desk and seek where birds are hiding in the trees. Feel wonder and gratitude as your benediction at the end of the day. I hope this small addition to your life becomes one of the most rewarding.

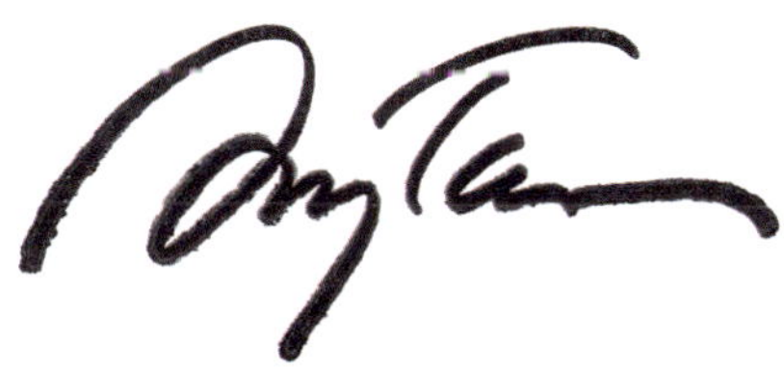

Personal Goals

Professional Goals

SUN	MON	TUE	WED	THU

FRI	SAT

MONTH

REMEMBER

NOTES

SUN	MON	TUE	WED	THU

FRI	SAT

MONTH

REMEMBER

NOTES

SUN	MON	TUE	WED	THU

FRI	SAT

MONTH

REMEMBER

NOTES

SUN	MON	TUE	WED	THU

FRI	SAT

MONTH

REMEMBER

NOTES

SUN	MON	TUE	WED	THU

FRI	SAT

MONTH

REMEMBER

NOTES

SUN MON TUE WED THU FRI SAT

Date: ______________ Weather: ______________

INTENTIONAL MOMENTS

MY DAY

Morning: ______________

Afternoon: ______________

Evening: ______________

SUN MON TUE WED THU FRI SAT

Date: ______________ Weather: ______________

INTENTIONAL MOMENTS

MY DAY

Morning: ______________

Afternoon: ______________

Evening: ______________

SUN MON TUE WED THU FRI SAT

Date: ______________ Weather: ______________

INTENTIONAL MOMENTS

MY DAY

Morning:

Afternoon:

Evening:

SUN MON TUE WED THU FRI SAT

Date: ______________ Weather: ______________

INTENTIONAL MOMENTS

MY DAY

Morning:

Afternoon:

Evening:

SUN MON TUE WED THU FRI SAT

Date: ______________ Weather: ______________

INTENTIONAL MOMENTS

MY DAY

Morning: ______________

Afternoon: ______________

Evening: ______________

SUN MON TUE WED THU FRI SAT

Date: ____________ Weather: ____________

INTENTIONAL MOMENTS

MY DAY

Morning:

Afternoon:

Evening:

SUN MON TUE WED THU FRI SAT

Date: ____________ Weather: ____________

INTENTIONAL MOMENTS

MY DAY

Morning: ____________

Afternoon: ____________

Evening: ____________

Reflections

As a child I discovered strange wonders by crawling over shrubs, pushing aside brambles . . . wading in water, and getting scratched up, banged up, or torn up. Let me return to childhood wonderment to discover more.

SUN MON TUE WED THU FRI SAT

Date: ____________ Weather: ____________

INTENTIONAL MOMENTS

MY DAY

Morning:

Afternoon:

Evening:

SUN MON TUE WED THU FRI SAT

Date: ______________ Weather: ______________

INTENTIONAL MOMENTS

MY DAY

Morning:

Afternoon:

Evening:

SUN MON TUE WED THU FRI SAT

Date: ____________ Weather: ____________

INTENTIONAL MOMENTS

MY DAY

Morning:

Afternoon:

Evening:

SUN MON TUE WED THU FRI SAT

Date: ____________ Weather: ____________

INTENTIONAL MOMENTS

MY DAY

Morning: ____________

Afternoon: ____________

Evening: ____________

SUN MON TUE WED THU FRI SAT

Date: ____________ Weather: ____________

INTENTIONAL MOMENTS

MY DAY

Morning:

Afternoon:

Evening:

SUN MON TUE WED THU FRI SAT

Date: ______________ Weather: ______________

INTENTIONAL MOMENTS

MY DAY

Morning:

Afternoon:

Evening:

SUN MON TUE WED THU FRI SAT

Date: ____________ Weather: ____________

INTENTIONAL MOMENTS

MY DAY

Morning:

Afternoon:

Evening:

Reflections

Questions that beget more questions are the fertile spores that can lead you deeper into the forest.

SUN MON TUE WED THU FRI SAT

Date: ____________ Weather: ____________

INTENTIONAL MOMENTS

MY DAY

Morning: ____________

Afternoon: ____________

Evening: ____________

SUN MON TUE WED THU FRI SAT

Date: ____________ Weather: ____________

INTENTIONAL MOMENTS

MY DAY

Morning:

Afternoon:

Evening:

SUN MON TUE WED THU FRI SAT

Date: ____________ Weather: ____________

INTENTIONAL MOMENTS

MY DAY

Morning: ____________

Afternoon: ____________

Evening: ____________

SUN MON TUE WED THU FRI SAT

Date: ____________ Weather: ____________

INTENTIONAL MOMENTS

MY DAY

Morning: ____________

Afternoon: ____________

Evening: ____________

SUN MON TUE WED THU FRI SAT

Date: ____________________ Weather: ____________________

INTENTIONAL MOMENTS

MY DAY

Morning: ____________________

Afternoon: ____________________

Evening: ____________________

SUN MON TUE WED THU FRI SAT

Date: ____________ Weather: ____________

INTENTIONAL MOMENTS

MY DAY

Morning: ____________

Afternoon: ____________

Evening: ____________

SUN MON TUE WED THU FRI SAT

Date: ______________ Weather: ______________

INTENTIONAL MOMENTS

MY DAY

Morning:

Afternoon:

Evening:

Reflections

Perfection can be the antithesis of spontaneity.

SUN MON TUE WED THU FRI SAT

Date: ____________ Weather: ____________

INTENTIONAL MOMENTS

MY DAY

Morning: ____________

Afternoon: ____________

Evening: ____________

SUN MON TUE WED THU FRI SAT

Date: ______________ Weather: ______________

INTENTIONAL MOMENTS

MY DAY

Morning: ______________

Afternoon: ______________

Evening: ______________

SUN MON TUE WED THU FRI SAT

Date: ____________ Weather: ____________

INTENTIONAL MOMENTS

MY DAY

Morning:

Afternoon:

Evening:

SUN MON TUE WED THU FRI SAT

Date: ______________ Weather: ______________

INTENTIONAL MOMENTS

MY DAY

Morning:

Afternoon:

Evening:

SUN MON TUE WED THU FRI SAT

Date: ____________ Weather: ____________

INTENTIONAL MOMENTS

MY DAY

Morning:

Afternoon:

Evening:

SUN MON TUE WED THU FRI SAT

Date: ______________ Weather: ______________________

INTENTIONAL MOMENTS

MY DAY

Morning: ______________________

Afternoon: ______________________

Evening: ______________________

SUN MON TUE WED THU FRI SAT

Date: ____________ Weather: ____________

INTENTIONAL MOMENTS

MY DAY

Morning:

Afternoon:

Evening:

Reflections

I love the mornings when I step out and all is quiet. As soon as I whistle, the birds call out—not singing prettily, but loudly calling.

SUN MON TUE WED THU FRI SAT

Date: ______________ Weather: ______________

INTENTIONAL MOMENTS

MY DAY

Morning:

Afternoon:

Evening:

SUN MON TUE WED THU FRI SAT

Date: ____________ Weather: ____________

INTENTIONAL MOMENTS

MY DAY

Morning:

Afternoon:

Evening:

SUN MON TUE WED THU FRI SAT

Date: ____________ Weather: ____________

INTENTIONAL MOMENTS

MY DAY

Morning: ____________

Afternoon: ____________

Evening: ____________

SUN MON TUE WED THU FRI SAT

Date: ______________ Weather: ______________________

INTENTIONAL MOMENTS

MY DAY

Morning: ______________________

Afternoon: ______________________

Evening: ______________________

SUN MON TUE WED THU FRI SAT

Date: ____________ Weather: ____________

INTENTIONAL MOMENTS

MY DAY

Morning:

Afternoon:

Evening:

SUN MON TUE WED THU FRI SAT

Date: ______________ Weather: ______________

INTENTIONAL MOMENTS

MY DAY

Morning:

Afternoon:

Evening:

SUN MON TUE WED THU FRI SAT

Date: ______________ Weather: ______________

INTENTIONAL MOMENTS

MY DAY

Morning:

Afternoon:

Evening:

Reflections

By disposition, I am an observer. I want to know why things happen. I need to feel the gut kick of strong emotions.

SUN MON TUE WED THU FRI SAT

Date: ____________ Weather: ____________

INTENTIONAL MOMENTS

MY DAY

Morning: ____________

Afternoon: ____________

Evening: ____________

SUN MON TUE WED THU FRI SAT

Date: ____________ Weather: ____________

INTENTIONAL MOMENTS

MY DAY

Morning:

Afternoon:

Evening:

SUN MON TUE WED THU FRI SAT

Date: ____________ Weather: ____________

INTENTIONAL MOMENTS

MY DAY

Morning: ____________

Afternoon: ____________

Evening: ____________

SUN MON TUE WED THU FRI SAT

Date: ______________________ Weather: ______________________

INTENTIONAL MOMENTS

MY DAY

Morning: ______________________

Afternoon: ______________________

Evening: ______________________

SUN MON TUE WED THU FRI SAT

Date: ____________ Weather: ____________

INTENTIONAL MOMENTS

MY DAY

Morning: ____________

Afternoon: ____________

Evening: ____________

SUN MON TUE WED THU FRI SAT

Date: ____________ Weather: ____________

INTENTIONAL MOMENTS

MY DAY

Morning: ____________

Afternoon: ____________

Evening: ____________

SUN MON TUE WED THU FRI SAT

Date: ____________ Weather: ____________

INTENTIONAL MOMENTS

MY DAY

Morning:

Afternoon:

Evening:

Reflections

The more I observe, the more I realize that every part of a bird and every behavior has a specific purpose, a reason, and individual meaning. Instinct does not account for everything that is fascinating.

SUN MON TUE WED THU FRI SAT

Date: ____________ Weather: ____________

INTENTIONAL MOMENTS

MY DAY

Morning:

Afternoon:

Evening:

SUN MON TUE WED THU FRI SAT

Date: ____________ Weather: ____________

INTENTIONAL MOMENTS

MY DAY

Morning:

Afternoon:

Evening:

SUN MON TUE WED THU FRI SAT

Date: ______________ Weather: ______________

INTENTIONAL MOMENTS

MY DAY

Morning:

Afternoon:

Evening:

SUN MON TUE WED THU FRI SAT

Date: ____________ Weather: ____________

INTENTIONAL MOMENTS

MY DAY

Morning: ____________

Afternoon: ____________

Evening: ____________

SUN MON TUE WED THU FRI SAT

Date: ____________ Weather: ____________

INTENTIONAL MOMENTS

MY DAY

Morning:

Afternoon:

Evening:

SUN MON TUE WED THU FRI SAT

Date: ____________ Weather: ____________

INTENTIONAL MOMENTS

MY DAY

Morning:

Afternoon:

Evening:

SUN MON TUE WED THU FRI SAT

Date: ____________ Weather: ____________

INTENTIONAL MOMENTS

MY DAY

Morning: ____________

Afternoon: ____________

Evening: ____________

Reflections

Every bird is a good bird to see, even the ones I see all the time. I am happy they've come, that they've chosen my yard to visit for a few minutes or the day or every day for many weeks or months.

SUN MON TUE WED THU FRI SAT

Date: ______________ Weather: ______________

INTENTIONAL MOMENTS

MY DAY

Morning: ______________

Afternoon: ______________

Evening: ______________

SUN MON TUE WED THU FRI SAT

Date: ____________ Weather: ____________

INTENTIONAL MOMENTS

MY DAY

Morning: ____________

Afternoon: ____________

Evening: ____________

SUN MON TUE WED THU FRI SAT

Date: ____________________ Weather: ____________________

INTENTIONAL MOMENTS

MY DAY

Morning: ____________________

Afternoon: ____________________

Evening: ____________________

SUN MON TUE WED THU FRI SAT

Date: ____________ Weather: ____________

INTENTIONAL MOMENTS

MY DAY

Morning: ____________

Afternoon: ____________

Evening: ____________

SUN MON TUE WED THU FRI SAT

Date: ____________________ Weather: ____________________

INTENTIONAL MOMENTS

MY DAY

Morning: ____________________

Afternoon: ____________________

Evening: ____________________

SUN MON TUE WED THU FRI SAT

Date: ______________ Weather: ______________

INTENTIONAL MOMENTS

MY DAY

Morning:

Afternoon:

Evening:

SUN MON TUE WED THU FRI SAT

Date: ____________ Weather: ____________

INTENTIONAL MOMENTS

MY DAY

Morning:

Afternoon:

Evening:

Reflections

I hope I never cease to be amazed.

SUN MON TUE WED THU FRI SAT

Date: ____________ Weather: ____________

INTENTIONAL MOMENTS

MY DAY

Morning:

Afternoon:

Evening:

SUN MON TUE WED THU FRI SAT

Date: ______________ Weather: ______________

INTENTIONAL MOMENTS

MY DAY

Morning: ______________

Afternoon: ______________

Evening: ______________

SUN MON TUE WED THU FRI SAT

Date: ____________ Weather: ____________

INTENTIONAL MOMENTS

MY DAY

Morning:

Afternoon:

Evening:

SUN MON TUE WED THU FRI SAT

Date: ______________ Weather: ______________

INTENTIONAL MOMENTS

MY DAY

Morning:

Afternoon:

Evening:

SUN MON TUE WED THU FRI SAT

Date: ____________ Weather: ____________

INTENTIONAL MOMENTS

MY DAY

Morning: ____________

Afternoon: ____________

Evening: ____________

SUN MON TUE WED THU FRI SAT

Date: ____________ Weather: ____________

INTENTIONAL MOMENTS

MY DAY

Morning:

Afternoon:

Evening:

SUN MON TUE WED THU FRI SAT

Date: ____________________ Weather: ____________________

INTENTIONAL MOMENTS

MY DAY

Morning: ____________________

Afternoon: ____________________

Evening: ____________________

Reflections

I am always happy to find exceptions to what I hastily judged to be the rule. Nature abhors a generalist.

SUN MON TUE WED THU FRI SAT

Date: ____________________ Weather: ____________________

INTENTIONAL MOMENTS

MY DAY

Morning: ____________________

Afternoon: ____________________

Evening: ____________________

SUN MON TUE WED THU FRI SAT

Date: ______________ Weather: ______________

INTENTIONAL MOMENTS

MY DAY

Morning:

Afternoon:

Evening:

SUN MON TUE WED THU FRI SAT

Date: ____________ Weather: ____________

INTENTIONAL MOMENTS

MY DAY

Morning: ____________

Afternoon: ____________

Evening: ____________

SUN MON TUE WED THU FRI SAT

Date: ____________ Weather: ____________

INTENTIONAL MOMENTS

MY DAY

Morning: ____________

Afternoon: ____________

Evening: ____________

SUN MON TUE WED THU FRI SAT

Date: ________ Weather: ________

INTENTIONAL MOMENTS

MY DAY

Morning:

Afternoon:

Evening:

SUN MON TUE WED THU FRI SAT

Date: ____________ Weather: ____________

INTENTIONAL MOMENTS

MY DAY

Morning:

Afternoon:

Evening:

SUN MON TUE WED THU FRI SAT

Date: ______________ Weather: ______________

INTENTIONAL MOMENTS

MY DAY

Morning:

Afternoon:

Evening:

Reflections

Each bird is surprising and thrilling in its own way. But the most special is the bird that pauses when it is eating, looks and acknowledges I am there, then goes back to what it was doing.

SUN MON TUE WED THU FRI SAT

Date: ____________ Weather: ____________

INTENTIONAL MOMENTS

MY DAY

Morning: ____________

Afternoon: ____________

Evening: ____________

SUN MON TUE WED THU FRI SAT

Date: ______________________ Weather: ______________________

INTENTIONAL MOMENTS

MY DAY

Morning: ______________________

Afternoon: ______________________

Evening: ______________________

SUN MON TUE WED THU FRI SAT

Date: ____________ Weather: ____________

INTENTIONAL MOMENTS

MY DAY

Morning: ____________

Afternoon: ____________

Evening: ____________

SUN MON TUE WED THU FRI SAT

Date: ____________ Weather: ____________

INTENTIONAL MOMENTS

MY DAY

Morning:

Afternoon:

Evening:

SUN MON TUE WED THU FRI SAT

Date: ____________ Weather: ____________

INTENTIONAL MOMENTS

MY DAY

Morning: ____________

Afternoon: ____________

Evening: ____________

SUN MON TUE WED THU FRI SAT

Date: ____________ Weather: ____________

INTENTIONAL MOMENTS

MY DAY

Morning: ____________

Afternoon: ____________

Evening: ____________

SUN MON TUE WED THU FRI SAT

Date: ____________ Weather: ____________

INTENTIONAL MOMENTS

MY DAY

Morning: ____________

Afternoon: ____________

Evening: ____________

Reflections

I'm a dependable human. Every bird says so.

SUN MON TUE WED THU FRI SAT

Date: ____________ Weather: ____________

INTENTIONAL MOMENTS

MY DAY

Morning: ____________

Afternoon: ____________

Evening: ____________

SUN MON TUE WED THU FRI SAT

Date: ____________ Weather: ____________

INTENTIONAL MOMENTS

MY DAY

Morning: ____________

Afternoon: ____________

Evening: ____________

SUN MON TUE WED THU FRI SAT

Date: ____________ Weather: ____________

INTENTIONAL MOMENTS

MY DAY

Morning:

Afternoon:

Evening:

SUN MON TUE WED THU FRI SAT

Date: ______________ Weather: ______________

INTENTIONAL MOMENTS

MY DAY

Morning:

Afternoon:

Evening:

SUN MON TUE WED THU FRI SAT

Date: ______________ Weather: ______________

INTENTIONAL MOMENTS

MY DAY

Morning: ______________

Afternoon: ______________

Evening: ______________

SUN MON TUE WED THU FRI SAT

Date: ______________ Weather: ______________

INTENTIONAL MOMENTS

MY DAY

Morning:

Afternoon:

Evening:

SUN MON TUE WED THU FRI SAT

Date: ______________ Weather: ______________

INTENTIONAL MOMENTS

MY DAY

Morning: ______________

Afternoon: ______________

Evening: ______________

Reflections

Embrace what John Muir Laws describes as "intentional curiosity," what leads us to deep observation and wonderment.

SUN MON TUE WED THU FRI SAT

Date: ____________ Weather: ____________

INTENTIONAL MOMENTS

MY DAY

Morning:

Afternoon:

Evening:

SUN MON TUE WED THU FRI SAT

Date: ______________________ Weather: ______________________________________

INTENTIONAL MOMENTS

MY DAY

Morning: ______________________________________

Afternoon: ______________________________________

Evening: ______________________________________

SUN MON TUE WED THU FRI SAT

Date: ____________ Weather: ____________

INTENTIONAL MOMENTS

MY DAY

Morning: ____________

Afternoon: ____________

Evening: ____________

SUN MON TUE WED THU FRI SAT

Date: ____________ Weather: ____________

INTENTIONAL MOMENTS

MY DAY

Morning:

Afternoon:

Evening:

SUN MON TUE WED THU FRI SAT

Date: ____________ Weather: ____________

INTENTIONAL MOMENTS

MY DAY

Morning:

Afternoon:

Evening:

SUN MON TUE WED THU FRI SAT

Date: ____________ Weather: ____________

INTENTIONAL MOMENTS

MY DAY

Morning:

Afternoon:

Evening:

SUN MON TUE WED THU FRI SAT

Date: ____________ Weather: ____________

INTENTIONAL MOMENTS

MY DAY

Morning: ____________

Afternoon: ____________

Evening: ____________

Reflections

Birds are creatures of habit in their habitat. Me, too.

SUN MON TUE WED THU FRI SAT

Date: ______________ Weather: ______________

INTENTIONAL MOMENTS

MY DAY

Morning:

Afternoon:

Evening:

SUN MON TUE WED THU FRI SAT

Date: ____________ Weather: ____________

INTENTIONAL MOMENTS

MY DAY

Morning:

Afternoon:

Evening:

SUN MON TUE WED THU FRI SAT

Date: ____________ Weather: ____________

INTENTIONAL MOMENTS

MY DAY

Morning:

Afternoon:

Evening:

SUN MON TUE WED THU FRI SAT

Date:

Weather:

INTENTIONAL MOMENTS

MY DAY

Morning:

Afternoon:

Evening:

SUN MON TUE WED THU FRI SAT

Date: ____________ Weather: ____________

INTENTIONAL MOMENTS

MY DAY

Morning:

Afternoon:

Evening:

SUN MON TUE WED THU FRI SAT

Date: ____________ Weather: ____________

INTENTIONAL MOMENTS

MY DAY

Morning: ____________

Afternoon: ____________

Evening: ____________

SUN MON TUE WED THU FRI SAT

Date: ____________ Weather: ____________

INTENTIONAL MOMENTS

MY DAY

Morning:

Afternoon:

Evening:

Reflections

By imagining I was that bird, I felt a personal connection to it and a deeper sense of what life is like for every bird: Each day is a chance to survive.

SUN MON TUE WED THU FRI SAT

Date: ______ Weather: ______

INTENTIONAL MOMENTS

MY DAY

Morning: ______

Afternoon: ______

Evening: ______

SUN MON TUE WED THU FRI SAT

Date: ______________ Weather: ______________

INTENTIONAL MOMENTS

MY DAY

Morning: ______________

Afternoon: ______________

Evening: ______________

SUN MON TUE WED THU FRI SAT

Date: ______________ Weather: ______________

INTENTIONAL MOMENTS

MY DAY

Morning: ______________

Afternoon: ______________

Evening: ______________

SUN MON TUE WED THU FRI SAT

Date: ____________ Weather: ____________

INTENTIONAL MOMENTS

MY DAY

Morning:

Afternoon:

Evening:

SUN MON TUE WED THU FRI SAT

Date: ____________________ Weather: ____________________

INTENTIONAL MOMENTS

MY DAY

Morning:

Afternoon:

Evening:

SUN MON TUE WED THU FRI SAT

Date: ______________________ Weather: ______________________

INTENTIONAL MOMENTS

MY DAY

Morning: ______________________

Afternoon: ______________________

Evening: ______________________

SUN MON TUE WED THU FRI SAT

Date: ____________ Weather: ____________

INTENTIONAL MOMENTS

MY DAY

Morning:

Afternoon:

Evening:

Reflections

With both fiction and birds, I think about existence, the span of life, from conception to birth to survival to death to remembrance by others.

SUN MON TUE WED THU FRI SAT

Date: ______________ Weather: ______________

INTENTIONAL MOMENTS

MY DAY

Morning: ______________

Afternoon: ______________

Evening: ______________

SUN MON TUE WED THU FRI SAT

Date: ______________ Weather: ______________

INTENTIONAL MOMENTS

MY DAY

Morning:

Afternoon:

Evening:

SUN MON TUE WED THU FRI SAT

Date: ______________ Weather: ______________

INTENTIONAL MOMENTS

MY DAY

Morning:

Afternoon:

Evening:

SUN MON TUE WED THU FRI SAT

Date: ____________________ Weather: ________________________________

INTENTIONAL MOMENTS

MY DAY

Morning:

Afternoon:

Evening:

SUN MON TUE WED THU FRI SAT

Date: ______________ Weather: ______________

INTENTIONAL MOMENTS

MY DAY

Morning:

Afternoon:

Evening:

SUN MON TUE WED THU FRI SAT

Date: ______________ Weather: ______________

INTENTIONAL MOMENTS

MY DAY

Morning:

Afternoon:

Evening:

SUN MON TUE WED THU FRI SAT

Date: ____________ Weather: ____________

INTENTIONAL MOMENTS

MY DAY

Morning: ____________

Afternoon: ____________

Evening: ____________

Reflections

I reflect on mortality, the strangeness of it, the inevitability. I do that daily, and not with dread, but with awareness that life contains ephemeral moments, which can be saved in words and images, there for pondering, for reviving the bird and my heart.

SUN MON TUE WED THU FRI SAT

Date: ____________ Weather: ____________

INTENTIONAL MOMENTS

MY DAY

Morning: ____________

Afternoon: ____________

Evening: ____________

SUN MON TUE WED THU FRI SAT

Date: ____________ Weather: ____________

INTENTIONAL MOMENTS

MY DAY

Morning: ____________

Afternoon: ____________

Evening: ____________

SUN MON TUE WED THU FRI SAT

Date: ____________ Weather: ____________

INTENTIONAL MOMENTS

MY DAY

Morning:

Afternoon:

Evening:

SUN MON TUE WED THU FRI SAT

Date: ____________ Weather: ____________

INTENTIONAL MOMENTS

MY DAY

Morning: ____________

Afternoon: ____________

Evening: ____________

SUN MON TUE WED THU FRI SAT

Date: ____________ Weather: ____________

INTENTIONAL MOMENTS

MY DAY

Morning: ____________

Afternoon: ____________

Evening: ____________

SUN MON TUE WED THU FRI SAT

Date: ______________ Weather: ______________

INTENTIONAL MOMENTS

MY DAY

Morning: ______________

Afternoon: ______________

Evening: ______________

SUN MON TUE WED THU FRI SAT

Date: ____________ Weather: ____________

INTENTIONAL MOMENTS

MY DAY

Morning:

Afternoon:

Evening:

Reflections

Birds are not at all simple. They do what is beyond my ken, what I can only imagine, unless science or reincarnation enables me to become a bird.

SUN MON TUE WED THU FRI SAT

Date: ____________________ Weather: ____________________

INTENTIONAL MOMENTS

MY DAY

Morning:

Afternoon:

Evening:

SUN MON TUE WED THU FRI SAT

Date: ____________ Weather: ____________

INTENTIONAL MOMENTS

MY DAY

Morning: ____________

Afternoon: ____________

Evening: ____________

SUN MON TUE WED THU FRI SAT

Date: ____________ Weather: ____________

INTENTIONAL MOMENTS

MY DAY

Morning:

Afternoon:

Evening:

SUN MON TUE WED THU FRI SAT

Date: ______________ Weather: ______________

INTENTIONAL MOMENTS

MY DAY

Morning:

Afternoon:

Evening:

SUN MON TUE WED THU FRI SAT

Date: ____________ Weather: ____________

INTENTIONAL MOMENTS

MY DAY

Morning:

Afternoon:

Evening:

SUN MON TUE WED THU FRI SAT

Date: ______________________ Weather: ______________________

INTENTIONAL MOMENTS

MY DAY

Morning: ______________________

Afternoon: ______________________

Evening: ______________________

SUN MON TUE WED THU FRI SAT

Date: ____________ Weather: ____________

INTENTIONAL MOMENTS

MY DAY

Morning: ____________

Afternoon: ____________

Evening: ____________

Reflections

Each day I look at the birds and they look at me. Each individual bird is different. Each individual has its personality.

SUN MON TUE WED THU FRI SAT

Date: ______________ Weather: ______________

INTENTIONAL MOMENTS

MY DAY

Morning:

Afternoon:

Evening:

SUN MON TUE WED THU FRI SAT

Date: ______________ Weather: ______________

INTENTIONAL MOMENTS

MY DAY

Morning: ______________

Afternoon: ______________

Evening: ______________

SUN MON TUE WED THU FRI SAT

Date: ____________ Weather: ____________

INTENTIONAL MOMENTS

MY DAY

Morning:

Afternoon:

Evening:

SUN MON TUE WED THU FRI SAT

Date: ____________ Weather: ____________

INTENTIONAL MOMENTS

MY DAY

Morning: ____________

Afternoon: ____________

Evening: ____________

SUN MON TUE WED THU FRI SAT

Date: ______________ Weather: ______________

INTENTIONAL MOMENTS

MY DAY

Morning: ______________

Afternoon: ______________

Evening: ______________

SUN MON TUE WED THU FRI SAT

Date: ____________ Weather: ____________

INTENTIONAL MOMENTS

MY DAY

Morning:

Afternoon:

Evening:

SUN MON TUE WED THU FRI SAT

Date: ____________ Weather: ____________

INTENTIONAL MOMENTS

MY DAY

Morning: ____________

Afternoon: ____________

Evening: ____________

Reflections

I love the mornings when I step out and all is quiet.
As soon as I whistle, the birds call out–not singing prettily,
but loudly calling . . . it's the noisy start of a new day.

SUN MON TUE WED THU FRI SAT

Date: ____________ Weather: ____________

INTENTIONAL MOMENTS

MY DAY

Morning: ____________

Afternoon: ____________

Evening: ____________

SUN MON TUE WED THU FRI SAT

Date: ______________ Weather: ______________

INTENTIONAL MOMENTS

MY DAY

Morning: ______________

Afternoon: ______________

Evening: ______________

SUN MON TUE WED THU FRI SAT

Date: ____________ Weather: ____________

INTENTIONAL MOMENTS

MY DAY

Morning:

Afternoon:

Evening:

SUN MON TUE WED THU FRI SAT

Date: ______________ Weather: ______________

INTENTIONAL MOMENTS

MY DAY

Morning: ______________

Afternoon: ______________

Evening: ______________

SUN MON TUE WED THU FRI SAT

Date: ____________ Weather: ____________

INTENTIONAL MOMENTS

MY DAY

Morning:

Afternoon:

Evening:

SUN MON TUE WED THU FRI SAT

Date: ____________ Weather: ____________

INTENTIONAL MOMENTS

MY DAY

Morning:

Afternoon:

Evening:

SUN MON TUE WED THU FRI SAT

Date: ____________ Weather: ____________

INTENTIONAL MOMENTS

MY DAY

Morning: ____________

Afternoon: ____________

Evening: ____________

Reflections

It is remarkable what birds can endure. It is tragic what they cannot.

Clarkson Potter/Publishers
An imprint of the Crown Publishing Group
A division of Penguin Random House LLC
1745 Broadway
New York, NY 10019
clarksonpotter.com
penguinrandomhouse.com

Library of Congress Cataloging-in-Publication Data is on file with the publisher.

ISBN 979-8-217-03479-6

Editor: Angelin Adams | Editorial assistant: Darian Keels
Designer: Madi Reyes
Production designer: Christina Self
Production editor: Serena Wang
Production: Luisa Francavilla and Kelli Tokos
Compositor: Nick Patton
Marketer: Chloe Aryeh

Designs based on the book design by Jenny Carrow.

Manufactured in Malaysia

10 9 8 7 6 5 4 3 2 1

First Edition

The authorized representative in the EU for product safety and compliance is Penguin Random House Ireland, Morrison Chambers, 32 Nassau Street, Dublin D02 YH68, Ireland, https://eu-contact.penguin.ie.